Made in the USA
Monee, IL
14 March 2022

92903096R00057